T0207592

FINDING OUR WAY:
A Guide to Deepening Spiritual Practice

SUSAN HAWKINS SAGER

BALBOA.PRESS
A DIVISION OF HAY HOUSE

Balboa Press books may be ordered through booksellers or by contacting:

Balboa Press
A Division of Hay House
1663 Liberty Drive
Bloomington, IN 47403
www.balboapress.com
844-682-1282

Because of the dynamic nature of the Internet, any web addresses or links contained in
this book may have changed since publication and may no longer be valid. The views
expressed in this work are solely those of the author and do not necessarily reflect the views
of the publisher, and the publisher hereby disclaims any responsibility for them.

The author of this book does not dispense medical advice or prescribe the use of any technique as a form of
treatment for physical, emotional, or medical problems without the advice of a physician, either directly or
indirectly. The intent of the author is only to offer information of a general nature to help you in your quest
for emotional and spiritual well-being. In the event you use any of the information in this book for yourself,
which is your constitutional right, the author and the publisher assume no responsibility for your actions.

Any people depicted in stock imagery provided by Getty Images are models,
and such images are being used for illustrative purposes only.
Certain stock imagery © Getty Images.

ISBN: 978-1-9822-6081-1 (sc)
ISBN: 978-1-9822-6082-8 (e)

Library of Congress Control Number: 2020925681

Print information available on the last page.

Balboa Press rev. date: 01/19/2021

Remembering
Ben Marz
and
Judy Waxman

May their memories be for blessing!

Contents

Introduction

In the time it takes to read this sentence, your life can change dramatically. Just think about the disruption that occurs with a serious diagnosis, an unexpected death, divorce, bankruptcy, family problems and break-ups. The list goes on. It feels like we are drowning, struggling to catch our next breath. What do we do then?

Our faith traditions offer a range of spiritual practices. These practices can calm and center us. They connect us to the deepest part of ourselves and God. They quiet the constant voice-over in our brains. Spiritual practice is an important resource. Yet, it is not some sort of insurance that guarantees that bad things will not happen. What it does give us is strength and solace, perspective, and the promise that no matter what happens, we are not alone.

But what if you do not belong to, or even believe in, a particular faith tradition? Spiritual practice belongs to everyone, whether or not they are religious in a conventional sense.

This is a way to use each day as an opportunity to focus on a specific spiritual practice. That spiritual practice becomes the theme for that day-- the focal point for what you think, what you do, and what you say. It becomes the lens through which you examine everything that shows up in your experience.

The purpose of this guide is to discover spiritual practice in a way you may never have been able to do.

- The format of this book is simple. Each day focuses on a particular spiritual practice. For the most part, these practices are based in the world's major religions. A brief explanation is offered; sometimes, with an example from one or more of the traditions.

- It does not matter which day of the week you begin on or which month. After each day's theme, there are a series of inner prompts, or questions, to provide you with an opportunity to reflect on your experience.

- Day Fifty-One to Fifty-Three give you the opportunity to cultivate your own spiritual practice. No doubt you would add some practices and delete others. Any listing will be incomplete. What would you like to add? There are so many values to choose from. Perhaps your list includes listening, reconciliation, remembrance, resilience, or trust.

- There are many names for our experience of the sacred in addition to the ones which our major religions use. Perhaps you like Holy One, Almighty, Spirit, Source, the One, or All That Is. Feel free to use whatever name feels comfortable to you.

- Spiritual practice is a lot like brushing your teeth, according to spiritual teacher, Jacob Glass. You have to keep at it to experience the difference it makes. It is not like you can brush your teeth once and then, it is over and done with. Brushing is a commitment you make. You can resent brushing your teeth if you would like. However, that resentment does not eliminate the actual need to brush.

- When we love something, it is easy to imagine practicing it. Yet, the reverse is also true. When we continually practice something, we come to rely on it. We want its ongoing presence precisely because we have come to love it.

- If you miss a time or two, just continue where you left off. No need for guilt or self-recrimination. No medals are given for feeling bad, so just process those feelings and let them go.

- Try to resist the temptation to do more than one page at a time. There is nothing that sacred about the order of these topics. It is just that rushing through the pages will not help you absorb the overall process any faster. Doing it daily is what reinforces your intention.

- Depending upon on how you view privacy, you may feel initially hesitant about writing anything at all. Don't let that feeling keep you from getting what you can out of this guide. Reflecting on a given topic allows you to make connections that you might not otherwise make.

- Research suggests that more we engage our five senses in any activity, the more likely our brain is to imprint it. This is why journaling can be so effective. It utilizes handwriting (a kinesthetic activity) along with auditory and visual stimulation. As you write something, you listen to the "voice" in your brain and then see the words on the paper. Keep this in mind as you cultivate your spiritual practice. How can you involve more of your senses? You might even want to try something outside your usual comfort zone and explore a new talent or even a less-used sensory modality.

- Never forget that everything you do is part of your spiritual practice. Your day may involve parenting, working online at home, or working with others at an office. Whatever it is, this is your opportunity to become more conscious and connected. Everyday events become cues to remind you of your commitment. Every time the telephone rings, you wash your hands, or find yourself at a traffic light, it is an opportunity to re-focus on God. Instead of seeing these events as interruptions, they become contributions.

Day One: Accountability

Accountability involves our willingness to take responsibility for our actions. With regard to our accountability, two questions come to mind: *1.) To whom are we accountable?* As spiritual beings, our primary accountability is always to the One who created us. We are also accountable to other people, as well as to the different communities to which we belong. *2.) For what are we accountable?* Often we feel overly-responsible for some things, yet fail to feel accountable when we really should. When we are accountable, we recognize the impact our behavior has on others. We no longer blame other people, the situation or God for our mistakes. We take responsibility for our own shortcomings as well as our strengths. Our accountability usually goes hand in hand with our level of integrity. *How do you rate your own level of accountability?*

Inner Prompts

- Up until now, what has been your overall experience of this?

- What has kept you from practicing it more deeply?

- How might you integrate it more fully?

- What additional insights do you have now?

Day Two: Affirmation

Affirmation allows us to counteract the negative programming that bombards us from all sides. Remember that words shape our experience of ourselves. There are so many spoken and unspoken messages out there. We grow up with all of them competing for space in our heads.

An affirmation is a short, positive statement that is used to replace our worn-out, negative thought patterns. Over time, affirmations reprogram those thought patterns. The words themselves are not as important as the feeling level, the conviction, and the inner realization they evoke. Some examples might include; "I chose joy in this moment," "I love myself unconditionally," "I forgive myself for being human," or "I am enough." There are many authors and books that can assist you with creating your own affirmations.

In addition to creating your own affirmations, you can read those in the wisdom literature of your own tradition. Read them as if they were written for you personally. The Twenty-Third Psalm, for example, is full of affirmations. *Begin by selecting a particular bit of programming you grew up with. What impact has it had over time? What affirmation would you like to replace it with?*

Inner Prompts

- Up until now, what has been your overall experience of this?

- What has kept you from practicing it more deeply?

- How might you integrate it more fully?

- What additional insights do you have now?

Day Three: Appreciation

Appreciation involves our recognition of the tremendous good that exists in someone or something. The more appreciation we have in our life, the greater attention we pay to what is positive. We are still sensitive to what is negative but we refuse to let that block the view of what is. It is sad when someone only appreciates the good in their lives in retrospect, and not at the time. *What are you missing out on that you could be appreciating right now?*

Inner Prompts

- Up until now, what has been your overall experience of this?

- What has kept you from practicing it more deeply?

- How might you integrate it more fully?

- What additional insights do you have now?

Day Four: Authenticity

Authenticity relates to genuineness. There's nothing added or artificial. Instead of revealing a pre-packaged version of yourself to others, you express your whole self appropriately. Authenticity is considered a spiritual value because we often try to cut the fabric of who are to conform with current fashion. When you recognize your innate being as spiritual, this no longer tempts you in the same way. *When have you embodied authenticity? What impact did your authenticity have on the situations you were in?*

Inner Prompts

- Up until now, what has been your overall experience of this?

- What has kept you from practicing it more deeply?

- How might you integrate it more fully?

- What additional insights do you have now?

Day Five: Blessing

A blessing refers to God's favor and protection. The theme of blessing is a personal favorite. This word is used in many ways. We have blessings, we offer them, and we can even become them. There are numerous examples of blessing in every major religion.

"Namaste" is a Hindu word of blessing, often said as a greeting. This one word condenses many others. In one translation, it reads, "I honor the place in you in which the Universe resides. When you are in that place in you and I am in that place in me, we are in the same place."

Among other things, Jewish tradition asks its followers to make a hundred blessings every day. Some people might consider that an unrealistic goal. Yet, this practice only offers a starting point. *What are your blessings? What blessings would you be willing to make, either out loud or silently?*

Inner Prompts

- Up until now, what has been your overall experience of this?

- What has kept you from practicing it more deeply?

- How might you integrate it more fully?

- What additional insights do you have now?

Day Six: Charity

What we give back to the world in terms of our time, talent and treasure is our charity. Different religious traditions call it by different names. Islam, for example, refers to charity as "giving alms" in English. This is considered one of the five pillars of that faith. In Judaism, the word *tzedakah* is the Hebrew word used to refer to charitable or righteous giving. *What are some unique contributions you can make to others?*

Inner Prompts

- Up until now, what has been your overall experience of this?

- What has kept you from practicing it more deeply?

- How might you integrate it more fully?

- What additional insights do you have now?

Day Seven: Cheerfulness

Cheerfulness refers to the outward expression of our happiness and joy. It can be undervalued as a spiritual practice. In fact, cheerfulness is often taken for granted. Yet, it takes a tremendous amount of discipline to commit to it and share it with others. Cheerfulness can be contagious, too. *How might your cheerfulness make a difference?*

Inner Prompts

- Up until now, what has been your overall experience of this?

- What has kept you from practicing it more deeply?

- How might you integrate it more fully?

- What additional insights do you have now?

Day Eight: Commitment

When we make a commitment, we make a promise. When life is littered with broken agreements, it is difficult to know exactly what is underneath the clutter. If you want to understand what you are truly committed to, reflect on how you spend your time and invest you energy. *What is your commitment to your spiritual life?*

Inner Prompts

- Up until now, what has been your overall experience of this?

- What has kept you from practicing it more deeply?

- How might you integrate it more fully?

- What additional insights do you have now?

Day Nine: Contemplation

Contemplation refers to the act of deep reflection or inner seeing. In a spiritual context, contemplation refers to our reflection on a particular image that reminds us of our relationship to the sacred, our immersion in an ideal, or our thinking about some words from a sacred or inspirational text. When we value something, we spend time thinking about it. *What have you spent time contemplating recently?*

Inner Prompts

- Up until now, what has been your overall experience of this?

- What has kept you from practicing it more deeply?

- How might you integrate it more fully?

- What additional insights do you have now?

Day Ten: Courage

Many consider courage to be the foundation of all other values. It is the precondition of any true change. Courage comes from the French word for the heart and involves bravery. It is usually defined as the "ability to do something that frightens one." *When have you faced your fears and done whatever was asked of you anyway?*

Courage is also defined as "strength in the face of pain or grief." This second definition is intriguing. *When have you shown strength in the face of pain or grief?*

Inner Prompts

- Up until now, what has been your overall experience of this?

- What has kept you from practicing it more deeply?

- How might you integrate it more fully?

- What additional insights do you have now?

Day Eleven: Discernment

Discernment involves our relying on divine wisdom as part of every decision process. Discernment is important, whether it is applied to a particular situation or to an overall understanding of oneself. A particularly interesting example of discernment is found in the Quaker community. Quakers believe that each individual has inner access to God and that a committed group of fellow Quakers can be particularly helpful in our discernment. American author, Parker Palmer shared about meeting with what the Quakers call a Clearness Committee. As a result of this work, Palmer turned down an intriguing job offer. It became clear that the job description had a tremendous appeal to his ego but not to his deeper self. *What has discernment looked like in your own life ?*

Inner Prompts

- Up until now, what has been your overall experience of this?

- What has kept you from practicing it more deeply?

- How might you integrate it more fully?

- What additional insights do you have now?

Day Twelve: Enthusiasm

Enthusiasm refers to our passion for something. The word "enthusiasm" comes from the ancient Greek and refers to a person possessed by the divine. When we feel enthusiastic, we feel in tune with creation itself. This excitement can lead us toward our soul's purpose. *Have you ever felt genuinely enthusiastic about something?*

Inner Prompts

- Up until now, what has been your overall experience of this?

- What has kept you from practicing it more deeply?

- How might you integrate it more fully?

- What additional insights do you have now?

Day Thirteen: Forgiveness

Forgiveness offers us freedom. We are no longer held hostage to the past. Anger and resentment no longer control us. All forgiveness starts with forgiveness of ourselves. When we are unable to forgive ourselves, it becomes harder to forgive others. Sometimes we need to forgive ourselves for being unable to forgive a particular situation yet.

This prayer from Buddhist tradition was offered by Angela Montano in an online class she taught and then adapted by this author.

Notice the emphasis on "confusions" in this prayer. When we can acknowledge our own and others' fundamental misunderstanding of life, it becomes a little bit easier for us to forgive.

If I have harmed others in any way,
either knowingly or unknowingly,
through my own confusions,
I ask their forgiveness.

If anyone has harmed me in any way,
either knowingly or unknowingly,
through their own confusions,
I forgive them.

If there is any situation
I am not yet ready to forgive,
either knowingly or unknowingly,
through my own confusions,
I forgive myself for not yet being ready to forgive.

And if I harm myself in any way,
belittle, berate or betray myself
either knowingly or unknowingly,
through my own confusions,
I forgive myself.

Inner Prompts

- Up until now, what has been your overall experience of this?

- What has kept you from practicing it more deeply?

- How might you integrate it more fully?

- What additional insights do you have now?

Day Fourteen: Grace

Grace involves an unexpected intervention of the divine in everyday experience. It manifests as a sudden coincidence that comes just when the individual needs it most. It cannot be predicted and it may feel like a miracle. When we read about a two-year-old surviving a fall from a high rise, we conclude that it must have been a miracle. However, it is no less of a miracle when parents are able to forgive someone involved in a hit and run with their child. Both are gifts of grace. The grace you have experienced may not have been as dramatic, but no doubt it was unmistakable, particularly with the inner growth it prompted. *What instance of grace has had an impact on you?*

Inner Prompts

- Up until now, what has been your overall experience of this?

- What has kept you from practicing it more deeply?

- How might you integrate it more fully?

- What additional insights do you have now?

Day Fifteen: Gratitude

As the medieval Christian mystic, Meister Eckhart, once wrote, "If the only prayer you ever say is 'thank you', it would be enough." Gratitude is so simple that it is easy to overlook, even though its impact is huge. It is a magnifying glass that helps us experience everything as a gift. It is easy enough to be grateful when everything is going well. However, it is also possible to be grateful in the midst of tremendous difficulty and challenge. Many people keep a gratitude journal to reflect on what they are thankful for each day

C.K. Chesterton noted that, "When it comes to life, the critical thing is whether you take things for granted or take them with gratitude." *What inspires gratitude in you?*

Inner Prompts

- Up until now, what has been your overall experience of this?

- What has kept you from practicing it more deeply?

- How might you integrate it more fully?

- What additional insights do you have now?

Day Sixteen: Hope

Hope is a conviction that anything is possible -- whether a fresh start or a second chance, or perhaps, something miraculous. Hope keeps us going when our bodies and minds want to give up. It is not a guarantee that things will work out as we wish. Nevertheless, hope keeps us pressing forward when nothing else will. As the Dalai Lama once said, "No matter what sort of difficulties or how painful or experience is, if we lose our hope, that is our real disaster." *When has hope prompted you to press on when you were tempted to give up?*

Inner Prompts

- Up until now, what has been your overall experience of this?

- What has kept you from practicing it more deeply?

- How might you integrate it more fully?

- What additional insights do you have now?

Day Seventeen: Hospitality

Hospitality involves our warm welcome and treatment of guests or strangers. How can we keep the door to our hearts open? Sometimes we prefer to sit inside alone or slam the door shut. Hospitality may look different depending upon the specific situation we are in. Nevertheless, it involves sharing who we are and what we have. No one is considered an outsider when it comes to caring and compassion. *Who has been your model of hospitality?*

Inner Prompts

- Up until now, what has been your overall experience of this?

- What has kept you from practicing it more deeply?

- How might you integrate it more fully?

- What additional insights do you have now?

Day Eighteen: Inner Inventory

An inner inventory allows us to be accountable and take stock of every aspect of our lives. One method is to take the time to ask ourselves questions and wait for the answer. Over time, our answer to the very same question may vary, letting us know how we have changed. Here are a few questions that might be helpful to you. Undoubtedly, you will come up with others. *What questions would you like to add?*

- What are your priorities? Take a moment to look at the way you currently use your time, energy and resources. Is that consistent with what you say your priorities are?

- Why do you think you are here? How has your answer to this question changed over time?

- Who and what do you love?

- What do you see as the gifts you have to give ?

- What image do you think you project to others? Does it really reflect who you are? Does your image hold you hostage?

- What is your shadow self? What do you continually resist in yourself and others? What is the gift your shadow has to give you?

Inner Prompts

- Up until now, what has been your overall experience of this?

- What has kept you from practicing it more deeply?

- How might you integrate it more fully?

- What additional insights do you have now?

Day Nineteen: Integrity

Acting with integrity involves choosing to live in accordance with one's values. It involves honesty and authenticity. Integrity requires us to act in alignment with what we believe. A number of values come together to create integrity; courage, decency, discernment, fairness, self-awareness and wisdom. *Think of a particular time when you demonstrated integrity.*

Inner Prompts

- Up until now, what has been your overall experience of this?

- What has kept you from practicing it more deeply?

- How might you integrate it more fully?

- What additional insights do you have now?

Day Twenty: Journaling

A journal is more than a diary that holds names, dates and events. It is also a profound spiritual practice that allows us to record and reflect on our deepest joys and challenges. Catholic nun, Joan Chittester once wrote that journals "refuse to let us hide from ourselves." Elsewhere she called journals "the X-rays of our souls." *Have you ever reread any earlier journals of yours? What did you learn about yourself from reading them?*

Inner Prompts

- Up until now, what has been your overall experience of this?

- What has kept you from practicing it more deeply?

- How might you integrate it more fully?

- What additional insights do you have now?

Day Twenty-One: Joy

Joy is defined as a profound sense of happiness. The good news is you do not have to wait for either your life, or our world, to be perfect to experience it. You can claim joy right now. It is not dependent on outer circumstances any more than gratitude is. Joy does not come and go. What comes and goes is your attunement to joy. It is always there, like a deep underground spring. waiting for you to tap into it.

Your joy matters! Not only is your joy a vital component of your own well-being, but also, research indicates that your joy has an impact on those around you. *What brings you joy?*

Inner Prompts

- Up until now, what has been your overall experience of this?

- What has kept you from practicing it more deeply?

- How might you integrate it more fully?

- What additional insights do you have now?

Day Twenty-Two: Justice

Justice involves our acting justly, fairly, and equitably. Versions of this famous commentary on justice are in both Jewish and Christian texts and are attributed to the Prophet Micah.

And what does the Lord
require of you
but to do justly,
to love mercy,
and to walk humbly with your God?

> *- Micah 6:8*
> *NKJV*

We live out justice in relation to others and ourselves. *When did your sense of justice take shape? Who has inspired you along the way?*

Inner Prompts

- Up until now, what has been your overall experience of this?

- What has kept you from practicing it more deeply?

- How might you integrate it more fully?

- What additional insights do you have now?

Day Twenty-Three: Laughter

Laughter is often the sound of joy. Something about laughter lifts and lightens us up. The life of Norman Cousins underscores this value.

Norman Cousins was a well-known American editor and critic who was born in 1915 and died in 1990. In 1965, he was diagnosed with a connective tissue disease and given a one-in-500 chance of survival. At the nadir of his illness, Cousins was immobile.

Cousins was inspired to take charge of his own recovery under continued medical supervision. As part of his treatment, he viewed several hours of comedy each day. Throughout his life, Cousins was known for his optimism, kindness and love of life.

He found that ten minutes of genuine belly laughter had an anesthetic effect that produced approximately two hours of pain-free sleep. As he said, "Hearty laughter is a good way to jog internally without having to go outdoors." Almost two years after he began this treatment, he was considered cured.

Subsequently, he wrote several best-selling books on illness and healing, including the 1979 classic, Anatomy of an Illness as Perceived by the Patient. He was also invited to serve on the faculty of the University of Southern California. He lived 25 years after his diagnosis and died at the age of 75.

What makes you laugh?

Inner Prompts

- Up until now, what has been your overall experience of this?

- What has kept you from practicing it more deeply?

- How might you integrate it more fully?

- What additional insights do you have now?

Day Twenty-Four: Love

In this context, love is the essence of unwavering devotion. It is the basis of every other spiritual practice. Imagine living in a space of unconditional love, forgiveness, and understanding; then, try to imagine what the source of this love would be like.

How do you imagine treating yourself? What if you truly loved yourself? What if you treated yourself with compassion or something approaching tenderness? What if you could forgive yourself? This forgiveness would not be a form of self-indulgence, by trying to excuse anything or explain it away. You would finally be "for-giving" love to yourself!

What if Divine Love was your permanent address rather than a temporary residence?

Inner Prompts

- Up until now, what has been your overall experience of this?

- What has kept you from practicing it more deeply?

- How might you integrate it more fully?

- What additional insights do you have now?

Day Twenty-Five: Loving-kindness

Loving-kindness focuses on our care and compassion for everyone including ourselves. In Buddhist tradition, the Metta Meditation is a 2,500 year-old meditation with loving-kindness as its theme. There are many translations. However, the author has used this one for over twenty-five years.

Its reference to "my own true nature" refers to our essential core being, which in the Buddhist view is our Buddha nature. The word "free" can mean whatever you want it to mean. Traditionally, it meant to be free from the illusion that we could ever be separate, since we are all inter-connected.

As you repeat these words with your inner voice, imagine your love and compassion spreading outward from yourself to those you love, and then, to all beings everywhere.

May I be at peace.
May my heart be open.
May I know the beauty of my own true nature.
May I be free.

May you be at peace.
May your heart be open.
May you know the beauty of your own true nature.
May you be free.

May we be at peace.
May our hearts be open.
May we know the beauty of our own true nature.
May we be free.

May all be at peace.
May all hearts be open.
May all know the beauty of their own true nature.
May all be free.

Inner Prompts

- Up until now, what has been your overall experience of this?

- What has kept you from practicing it more deeply?

- How might you integrate it more fully?

- What additional insights do you have now?

Day Twenty-Six: Meditation

Meditation uses a range of techniques to focus awareness and achieve an overall sense of calm and well-being. If prayer is how we speak to Spirit, then meditation allows space for the answer. The process can be as simple or complex as you want it to be. Try to let go of any expectations of how the process should be. If you have never meditated before, be kind to yourself. In fact, be kind to yourself, anyway! Commit to doing meditation on a regular basis, and find a time that works for you. The following are some guidelines that you may wish to use.

- Scan your body and note if you are uncomfortable or in pain. Readjust if necessary. Feel free to loosen any clothing that is restrictive, and also, to take off your shoes. Do not let your position become a distraction.

- Take five deep breaths, taking the time to slowly inhale and exhale. During the last exhalation, close your eyes. Use this time to let go of anything you may have been holding onto.

- If emotions come up, allow them to float by like clouds in the sky.

- Say a sacred word or phrase to yourself or perhaps, visualize something sacred. You can repeat something as simple as "joy", "love" or "peace". If other thoughts arise, just let them go. Over time, doing this will have a consistent, incremental effect on you.

- When you are ready, finish this part of your meditation with words of thanks to God for these moments together.

- Be conscious of your breathing again. Then feel yourself inside your body in a particular room. As you feel ready, reintroduce some movement. Meditation creates a pause in your day, so allow yourself to feel it.

There are many sort of meditations for you to try. Today you might try a walking meditation and feel each foot as it hits the ground. Notice the breeze on your face. How is this experience for you?

Inner Prompts

- Up until now, what has been your overall experience of this?

- What has kept you from practicing it more deeply?

- How might you integrate it more fully?

- What additional insights do you have now?

Day Twenty-Seven: Mindful Breathing

Breathing exercises are common across the major religions. The pace of our breathing as well as the depth of each breath affects how we feel physically and emotionally.

When we are under stress, we tend to take more shallow breaths. Many folks tend to hold their breath unconsciously. When we take shallow breaths, less oxygen gets circulated. And the less oxygen that gets circulated, the more sluggish and out-of-sorts we feel. This only underscores any negative feelings we may already have.

Breathe in for a count of five.
Hold your breath for a count of five.
Now breathe out for a count of five.

When you do this, you'll notice, if just for a moment that the very act of breathing centers you. Perhaps it even energizes you. Sometimes, that little bit is all you need to shift the way you are feeling.

A technique that helps you feel the immediate impact of your oxygen intake is called power breathing.

Press one nostril closed (it doesn't matter which one);
and inhale through the other nostril.
Now close the nostril you've been breathing through,
and exhale through the one that had been closed.
Repeat with both nostrils.

Take the time to notice your breath at different points throughout the day. Then, take another moment to consciously breathe more deeply. *This is one of the most important practices you can develop.* Combining deep breathing with relaxation techniques can really assist in shifting and softening your mood.

The Buddhist monk. Thich Nhat Hanh, suggested that we state an intention for each inhalation and exhalation. You can choose whatever works for you. Here is an example:

"Breathing in, I take in (peace)",
"Breathing out, I let out (tension)".

Inner Prompts

- Up until now, what has been your overall experience of this?

- What has kept you from practicing it more deeply?

- How might you integrate it more fully?

- What additional insights do you have now?

Day Twenty-Eight: Mindful Eating

There are so many choices involved with mindful eating: choosing whether or not to eat; deciding upon a particular way of eating (among them, vegetarian, vegan, kosher and halal); eating certain foods on special days; blessing your food before or after eating it. The list goes on.

What makes this such a useful discipline is that we come back to it again and again. Eating is something we have to do to survive. By making this a spiritual practice as well as an act of survival, we reinforce our values with each bite. *What does your way of eating suggest about your values?*

Inner Prompts

- Up until now, what has been your overall experience of this?

- What has kept you from practicing it more deeply?

- How might you integrate it more fully?

- What additional insights do you have now?

Day Twenty-Nine: Nature

The most fundamental part of us is called "human nature." We often consider nature "outside.' Sometimes, though, we are blessed to have the outside come inside. We can never forget our connection with nature and with the One who created it. Make it a priority to spend time outdoors in nature. You will never be sorry that you did. Do not wait to schedule your time in nature until you have spare time. That ensures that you will never be able to do it. Many feel a communion with Spirit while in nature. Nature has a lot to teach us but its lessons are wordless. *What are some of the lessons nature has taught you?*

Inner Prompts

- Up until now, what has been your overall experience of this?

- What has kept you from practicing it more deeply?

- How might you integrate it more fully?

- What additional insights do you have now?

Day Thirty: Openness

Openness is defined by your receptivity and acceptance. How open are you to people …to ideas …to God? The noise of the world and its distractions can drown out the still small voice. It would be easy to make life decisions based on something that happened decades ago. Do you really want to live your adult life based on decisions you made as a child or teenager? Yet many people do this when it comes to their spirituality. Openness places us squarely in the present and not in the past. *Are you open to what the universe is saying to you right now?*

Inner Prompts

- Up until now, what has been your overall experience of this?

- What has kept you from practicing it more deeply?

- How might you integrate it more fully?

- What additional insights do you have now?

Day Thirty-One: Patience

Patience refers to our forbearance, endurance, and our willingness to wait. It is easy to get stuck in the quicksand of "I want to be somewhere else--do something else--be someone else." And it is also easy to be impatient with ourselves for our own impatience. "What's the matter with me? I shouldn't be feeling so irritated/agitated/annoyed/restless."

Consider nature for a moment. It is a lesson in the meaning of patience. A seed needs to be planted; then it germinates and starts to sprout. Finally it becomes a full-grown flower. Nothing speeds up that process naturally.

As an antidote to impatience, try anchoring yourself in this present moment and then slow down your breathing. Then repeat that in the next moment and the next. *In fact, make a list for yourself of those things that seem to trigger your own impatience. Be sure to also list those times when you have succeeded in being patient.*

Inner Prompts

- Up until now, what has been your overall experience of this?

- What has kept you from practicing it more deeply?

- How might you integrate it more fully?

- What additional insights do you have now?

Day Thirty-Two: Peace

Peace involves an unshakeable sense of calm and tranquility. It implies wholeness and totality. It is interesting that peace is often defined as the absence of conflict. Yet, if we wait until then to experience peace, we may never achieve it. Our sense of peace is not dependent upon anything external. When you feel peace with yourself, you are content to be who you are and who you are not. While you prefer the world to live in harmony and without violence, you do not need those things to experience inner peace. *How important is peace to you?*

Inner Prompts

- Up until now, what has been your overall experience of this?

- What has kept you from practicing it more deeply?

- How might you integrate it more fully?

- What additional insights do you have now?

Day Thirty-Three: Pilgrimage

A pilgrimage involves a journey to a holy place in search of spiritual development. In Islam, the notion of a *Hadj,* or pilgrimage, is considered one of the four tenets of that faith. Over the past several centuries, the idea of pilgrimage has expanded to include an inner journey as well. *Have you ever to been to a sacred site? What was its effect on you?*

Inner Prompts

- Up until now, what has been your overall experience of this?

- What has kept you from practicing it more deeply?

- How might you integrate it more fully?

- What additional insights do you have now?

Day Thirty-Four: Prayer

Prayer involves our conversation with God. Like all conversations, it involves a whole range of circumstances. The late Dr. William Braud, a leading figure in consciousness research, studied prayer across cultures and identified a number of factors that he felt contributed to the sheer impact prayer has.

Attention: St. Theresa of Avila described the mind as a bucking bronco, difficult to train. Nevertheless, we can train ourselves to focus our attention. This sort of focus also involves our bonding with whomever or whatever we are praying for, as well as our bonding with the One to whom we direct our prayers. Unity is the goal.

Imagery and visualization: These two words are often used interchangeably, but actually, they convey different concepts. Both rely on pictures rather than words. Visualization involves pictures that we choose. The same visualization may not work for everyone. Think of the boy who used an image of Pac-Man gobbling up ghosts to help heal his cancer cells. This image did not work for a middle-aged pacifist. While we choose our visualizations, imagery seems to choose us. According to the late Dr. Carl Jung, the collective unconscious offers images with both universal and subjective meaning. Our task involves learning the language of our own personal symbolism.

Intention: In America, we tend to view intention as a form of willpower, a steamroller pushing us towards a given result. In other cultures, intention is seen as a way of aligning all aspects of our being (mind/body/spirit). It is the effortless Zen notion of "doing without doing."

Strong positive emotion: We need to focus on our love, compassion and feeling of oneness rather than any feelings of fear, worry or despair. Strong emotion creates some an energetic momentum. "Strong" does not mean forceful or aggressive. It can be inward and quiet. The ocean has deep currents do not disturb the surface, yet that does not diminish their power.

Prayer is
sitting in the silence
until it silences us,
choosing gratitude
until we are grateful,
and praising God
until we ourselves are an act of praise.
                        - Father Richard Rohr

Inner Prompts

- Up until now, what has been your overall experience of this?

- What has kept you from practicing it more deeply?

- How might you integrate it more fully?

- What additional insights do you have now?

Day Thirty-Five: Purpose

Our purpose refers to our underlying intention and motivation. Perhaps we wonder what on earth we are here for? Some people seem to know their purpose from a young age, while others search for it over a lifetime. It may even look like your purpose in life is what you are doing at a particular point: perhaps getting your education, working at a job, or raising your family. Yet, purpose focuses on our *being* as well as our *doing*. Purpose involves aligning our deepest values with what we do, so that what we do becomes an expression of who we are. *What do you see as your purpose in life?*

Inner Prompts

- Up until now, what has been your overall experience of this?

- What has kept you from practicing it more deeply?

- How might you integrate it more fully?

- What additional insights do you have now?

Day Thirty-Six: Respect

Respect involves our deep-seated regard for others. The essence of respect is that we value others apart from their utility to us.

Acceptance is key. We accept that we may not always agree or even like others. Respect may not come naturally. In which case, we need to cultivate it. *How has your view of respect changed over time?*

Inner Prompts

- Up until now, what has been your overall experience of this?

- What has kept you from practicing it more deeply?

- How might you integrate it more fully?

- What additional insights do you have now?

Day Thirty-Seven: Retreat

A retreat involves stepping back from our usual reality to focus on a deeper part of ourselves. Unlike a pilgrimage, it does not require a visit to a holy site. A retreat begins with the recognition that to go outward, we must first go within. We extract ourselves from everyday life to retrieve our perspective. Individuals come to a retreat looking for very different things: clarity, balance, a solution for a particular problem, perhaps an insight into a particular situation. Sometimes a retreat provides answers to questions that we did not even know were there. Away from the constant noise of the world, you can finally listen to what your heart is telling you, what your body is saying, and what the universe is communicating. You might plan to bring along a journal to jot down any discoveries. *Is a retreat something that interests you?*

Inner Prompts

- Up until now, what has been your overall experience of this?

- What has kept you from practicing it more deeply?

- How might you integrate it more fully?

- What additional insights do you have now?

Day Thirty-Eight: Reverence

Reverence involves our deep respect and regard for our Creator as well as what was created. An interesting example of respect is the life of Dr. Albert Schweitzer who lived from 1875-1965. Among other things, he was a Protestant missionary in Africa who won the Nobel Prize in 1952. He was also a theologian and author who challenged several Christian views. Many feel that challenging the word of God, or a particular view of God, is the antithesis of reverence. A deeply religious man, Dr. Schweitzer did not see it this way. Dr. Schweitzer is best known for his philosophy of 'reverence for life', which he believed should be the basis of how we treat everything around us. Dr. Schweitzer would not step on a mosquito or move an ant colony, if it were in the way of something he wanted to build. While we may not wish to follow him on these examples, there is still a much larger message for us to understand. *How do you express reverence in your daily life?*

Inner Prompts

- Up until now, what has been your overall experience of this?

- What has kept you from practicing it more deeply?

- How might you integrate it more fully?

- What additional insights do you have now?

Day Thirty-Nine: Ritual

Ritual is defined as a sacred rite. We are often starved for sacred ritual without even knowing it. We hunger for its consistency, along with how ritual provides us with both meaning and metaphors. Every age and stage of life involves its own rituals. Think of how your own tradition handles birth, coming of age, marriage, and death, among other events.

Sacred ritual requires us to pay attention and appreciate this particular moment we are in as opposed to the 1.440 other minutes in a day.

What rituals have made your life meaningful?

Inner Prompts

- Up until now, what has been your overall experience of this?

- What has kept you from practicing it more deeply?

- How might you integrate it more fully?

- What additional insights do you have now?

Day Forty: Sacred Art

Sacred art involves using our creative expression to honor the divine. It would be impossible to catalogue, much less comment on, all the sacred art that has been created across the world throughout time.

It is not likely that you have ever heard of Jeffrey Mallon and yet his contributions are no less meaningful. He lives and works in Austin, Texas, where he creates what he calls "offerings." Mallon's offerings are made of found materials, such as leaves, flowers and pebbles. He arranges these materials in small areas, often no larger than six inches wide, so that others can find them along with their own inspiration.

Austin is also home to Laura Zeiner. Among other things, she engraves tiny hearts on rocks and shells, and then, writes on them in even smaller silver letters, "Please take me!"

Use today to create your own form of sacred art. If you are not used to creating art, you might want to start by creating an "offering" of your own.

Inner Prompts

- Up until now, what has been your overall experience of this?

- What has kept you from practicing it more deeply?

- How might you integrate it more fully?

- What additional insights do you have now?

Day Forty-One: Sacred Movement

Sacred movement involves intentionally moving the body to honor the divine. Examples of sacred movement include everything from whirling dervishes to dance ministries. *Use this time to create a sequence of movements to honor the sacred. You might also choose to learn your favorite prayer or quote in sign language.*

Inner Prompts

- Up until now, what has been your overall experience of this?

- What has kept you from practicing it more deeply?

- How might you integrate it more fully?

- What additional insights do you have now?

Day Forty-Two: Sacred Sound

Sacred sound involves listening to or making sound that honors the divine. Activities include listening to sacred music, singing, chanting, reciting sacred sounds and more. What is important is how you make this theme relevant to your own life. *Perhaps you can sing your prayers today or set aside time to listen to and reflect upon a particular piece of sacred music.*

Inner Prompts

- Up until now, what has been your overall experience of this?

- What has kept you from practicing it more deeply?

- How might you integrate it more fully?

- What additional insights do you have now?

Day Forty-Three: Sacred Study

Each major religion has its own "Required Reading List" of sacred texts. Reading for your own inspiration is also important, whether or not it has ties to a particular religion. The satisfaction of spiritual study might even be called pleasurable, even though we usually consider satisfaction as something physical. In this context, we discover that satisfaction goes way beyond its usual definition. *Do you find sacred study satisfying?*

Inner Prompts

- Up until now, what has been your overall experience of this?

- What has kept you from practicing it more deeply?

- How might you integrate it more fully?

- What additional insights do you have now?

Day Forty-Four: Sanctifying Time

The idea of sanctifying time is a relatively new one. In ancient times, humanity made people or places sacred, but time was considered too abstract a concept. In contrast, Judaism believes that God sanctified the celebration of the seventh day, the Sabbath, as part of the Ten Commandments. Christianity and Islam also came to believe that the sabbath is sacred, although these faiths celebrate it on different days.

Some people even experience a particular moment in time as sacred, such as their wedding, the birth of a child, or perhaps, some moment in nature. *What moments do you consider sacred, as opposed to special?*

Inner Prompts

- Up until now, what has been your overall experience of this?

- What has kept you from practicing it more deeply?

- How might you integrate it more fully?

- What additional insights do you have now?

Day Forty-Five: Silence

Silence involves quiet and stillness. Seekers from all spiritual traditions are known to take vows of silence so that they are not interrupted by any distractions during their spiritual work. Silence permits the kind of reflection that goes beyond mere introspection. It allows you to be more sensitive to the flow of the divine. *How often do you enter into silence?*

Inner Prompts

- Up until now, what has been your overall experience of this?

- What has kept you from practicing it more deeply?

- How might you integrate it more fully?

- What additional insights do you have now?

Day Forty-Six: Simplicity

"Live simply that others may simply live" is a quote that has been attributed to Gandhi and Mother Theresa, as well as, St. Elizabeth Ann Seton. It is uncertain who actually said it but all three of them had lives that were deeply transformative. Embracing simplicity involves seeing life in a way that does not focus on our material goods. We find that we have more freedom when we have things, rather than our things having us. *What would simplicity look like in your life?*

Inner Prompts

- Up until now, what has been your overall experience of this?

- What has kept you from practicing it more deeply?

- How might you integrate it more fully?

- What additional insights do you have now?

Day Forty-Seven: Values

Values refer to the ideals that we hold dear, our guiding principles. Values inform our thoughts, words, and deeds. American thinkers from Benjamin Franklin to Brené Brown, as well as every major religious tradition, have advocated the importance of identifying our values and living by them.

Spiritual practice begins with choosing a specific value and then cultivating it. A value becomes a spiritual practice when we identify its importance, and then, flesh it out with some structure — perhaps a prayer, meditation, or reading, Finally, we add our own personal commitment to make sure it happens. *What values are particularly important to you?*

Inner Prompts

- Up until now, what has been your overall experience of this?

- What has kept you from practicing it more deeply?

- How might you integrate it more fully?

- What additional insights do you have now?

Day Forty-Eight: Wholeheartedness

Wholeheartedness is about integration. It is about bringing together our feelings, thoughts and actions in a way that allows us to be truly whole. Our culture has historically viewed vulnerability as a liability. Wholeheartedness assumes our underlying worthiness, no matter what our flaws are. *Who has been your example of wholeheartedness?*

Inner Prompts

- Up until now, what has been your overall experience of this?

- What has kept you from practicing it more deeply?

- How might you integrate it more fully?

- What additional insights do you have now?

Day Forty-Nine: Wisdom

Wisdom is intelligence combined with understanding, experience, and good judgement. It is not a matter of a high IQ or a stack of diplomas. A prime example of wisdom is King Solomon who was acknowledged in the sacred texts of Judaism, Christianity, and Islam. In one well-known story, King Solomon was asked to judge which of two women was the real mother of a baby. Both sides made a compelling case. King Solomon suggested that the baby be split with a sword, and that each woman be given half. One of the women protested, not wanting the baby to die in the process. King Solomon recognized the depth of her love and gave the baby to her. This was not just a clever solution to a dilemma; it demonstrated King Solomon's wisdom. Wisdom is free to acknowledge what it does not know, as well as what it does. *What example of wisdom particularly inspires you?*

Inner Prompts

- Up until now, what has been your overall experience of this?

- What has kept you from practicing it more deeply?

- How might you integrate it more fully?

- What additional insights do you have now?

Day Fifty: Wonder

Wonder involves our sense of reverential respect, surprise and awe. In a spiritual context, wonder often leads us to oneness and transcendence. It is important to cultivate our sense of wonder by being attentive to the mystery and miracles around us. This does not require us to shut our eyes to the injustice around us. Just make sure to also notice and appreciate the wonder. *Do you make sure you have a daily dose of wonder?*

Inner Prompts

- Up until now, what has been your overall experience of this?

- What has kept you from practicing it more deeply?

- How might you integrate it more fully?

- What additional insights do you have now?

Day Fifty-One: Cultivating Your Own

Inner Prompts

- Up until now, what has been your overall experience of this?

- What has kept you from practicing it more deeply?

- How might you integrate it more fully?

- What additional insights do you have now?

Day Fifty-Two: Cultivating Your Own

Inner Prompts

- Up until now, what has been your overall experience of this?

- What has kept you from practicing it more deeply?

- How might you integrate it more fully?

- What additional insights do you have now?

Day Fifty-Three: Cultivating Your Own

Inner Prompts

- Up until now, what has been your overall experience of this?

- What has kept you from practicing it more deeply?

- How might you integrate it more fully?

- What additional insights do you have now?

Acknowledgements

Nothing I have written here is as meaningful as the words you have added from your own experience. Thank you for choosing this book. And more than that, thank you for your presence here!

In 2013, a very different version of this material was created when a friend to many of us, Judy Waxman, was told to undergo a stem-cell transplant. Everyone who knew her wanted to do something. Judy was in isolation in a strange city, so I created 30 days-worth of reflections to accompany her.

Sometime later, I asked Dr. Ben Marz for his thoughts on what I had written. Ben had been dealing with a serious diagnosis of his own and offered tremendous warmth and wisdom, along with his own experience as a psychologist.

In the face of their difficult life experiences, both Judy's courage and determination, and Ben's positivity and sense of humor, had a profound impact. Sadly, they are both gone now. Their legacy continues to inspire others, as well as myself.

It was not until several years later, though, that current events inspired me to write the book that you are holding. Creating it gave me a focus during an incredibly difficult time. More than that, it underscored the role spiritual practice plays in grounding us and giving us strength. Perhaps the greatest gift it gave me was the continual reminder that I am never alone. God is always with me. God is always with you, too, even when it does not seem that way.

My gratitude goes out to everyone who has inspired me on this journey. I am especially grateful to my twin sister, Debora and her husband, Rev. Bob Perry. Debora was convinced I had a book in me and here it is! I am so grateful I followed her suggestion to reread earlier columns of mine as well as some other pieces I had written. I am grateful to the rest of our family as well: to our sister, Sara Hawkins Curtiss and to the memory of our parents, Phyllis and Dale Hawkins. I just wish my parents could have seen it. My gratitude also goes to my sister and brother-in-law, Karen and David Sager.

Thank you to everyone in my Torah study group, #TuesdayswithTrepp. It meant the world to be inspired by Rabbi Moshe and his wife Faigy each week. I deeply appreciate Judy Sorin's vision in starting this group!

I will never forget Debbie and Bill Brink for their encouragement and support over many years! Debbie, your belief in me carried me when I was not always so sure I believed in myself. And thank you to Chris Tedrow for opening your home and heart to me in the way that you have!

Understandably, my heartfelt gratitude belongs to my immediate family. I want to acknowledge my husband, Alan, who supported my writing and the long hours it took to put this book together. Our children--Erica and Ken Pelman, Jessica Sager, Rebecca Sager, Jacob Sager and Mira Lynn--all gave me encouragement and support during this process. Our grandchildren —Micah, Raviv, Tzvi, Neora, Remez, Shiraz and Ziv and Zeri -- are always an inspiration!

Gratitude to one and all and to the One Who Is All.

Susan Hawkins Sager
Austin, Texas

Printed in the United States
By Bookmasters